AIRBNB EIN Only

BOSSES BUILD BUSINESS CREDIT SERIES
VOLUME 2

PATRICE S. JORDAN

Airbnb EIN ONLY

Business Development & No PG Business Credit
Patrice S. Jordan, No PG Business Credit Consultant
www.Patricebookoffer.com

Key people to have as part of your business:

Renee Bobb, CEO of Renee Bobb Training LLC (https://reneebobbtraining.com/)
(Everything and more you need to know to win grants.)

Rosezena J. Pierce of RJ Pierce Law Group, P.C.
Trademark Attorney @thebizlawyer

ISBN: 979-8-9908768-1-1

Library of Congress Control Number: 2024914740

Printed in the United States

DEDICATION

To my dearest daughter, Lily,

You are the light that guided me through my darkest times. Your birth gave me the strength I needed to escape a life of domestic violence. Without you, I might not have had the courage to leave, or worse, I might not be here today. This book is for you, my love. I am forever grateful and endlessly proud to be your mother. I love you and thank you from the depths of my heart.

I also want to express my deepest gratitude to God. Thank you for carrying me through those challenging moments and placing me in a position where I can now extend a helping hand to those in need. Your guidance and strength have been my foundation.

ACKNOWLEDGMENTS

I would like to extend my heartfelt gratitude to those who have played significant roles in my journey.

First and foremost, to my sister, Louett Brown, thank you for providing me with a couch to sleep on when I needed it the most. Your support and kindness during my toughest times have been invaluable.

To my parents, Louis Jordan and Patricia Lowery, thank you for giving me life and for your unwavering love and support.

Most importantly, to my community, thank you for allowing me to lead you into continuous success. Your trust and support have been the foundation of my mission to empower and uplift.

WHAT TO EXPECT FROM THIS BOOK

"Thank you, coach! In the words of Kevin Hart, it's about to go down $5,000 to furnish my Airbnb." – *Hayne Ashley*

"Downtown Birmingham AIRBNB. Thank you, Patrice S. Jordan." – *Zaynab Mujahid*

"When I tell y'all Patrice is the goat, I mean that. I purchased the book last week and just got approved for my first property five minutes ago for Vegas. The move-in date is May 10th." – *Tee*

"Hey, boss babes! Thank you again, coach Patrice S. Jordan for putting me on to an entirely different game! Corporate lease is signed, beginning walk-through photos, transition videos coming." – *Moody Kat*

"Coach, I am nervous. I just posted my listing an hour ago and someone booked for twenty-eight days. God is good. I have a total of three units, and my goal is to have five this year! I was approved for two units in two days." – *April Grayson*

MEET THE AUTHOR

Patrice S. Jordan is the President of Her Secret Vault/ Bosses Build Business Credit. She is a well-known business credit expert, business consultant, and entrepreneur. With over ten years of entrepreneurial experience in many different areas of business, Patrice has become recognized as an authority in business credit building, acquiring business vehicles with no personal guarantee (PG), business consulting, and business credit scoring.

She has a passion for people and is dedicated to sharing her knowledge. Patrice is inspired by the community. She creates mentorship opportunities for those who need help in their business. These include building business credit, funding ideas, creating structure, gaining no PG vehicles, as well as so much more.

Her goal has always been to help people create multiple streams of income and provide them with a hub of knowledge. Patrice loves to better educate other business professionals because she believes everyone deserves to win.

CONTENTS

1

THE PERFECT BUSINESS STRUCTURE

The first thing we are going to talk about is structuring your business. Now, you may be thinking: *Why are we starting here?* Well, I'm about to tell you exactly why.

You see, when it comes to building your business credit, the lenders you will be seeking to open business credit accounts with (banks, vendors, auto dealerships, corporate leasing companies, etc.) want to see that you have a legitimate business which is *structured and set up correctly.*

I want you to remember one thing as you start to learn and understand what I am sharing with you—and as you get deeper into this book—one of the key principles of business credit is not just *what* you get approved for, but also *how much* you get approved for. Before we move on, I want to emphasize: **It**

is important to master this section before doing/applying anything else in the rest of this book.

I have carefully laid out this information in a specific order to teach you the fundamentals so that you can set up your business correctly. In this book I am not only teaching you *what* to do and *how* to do it but also *when* to do it! This is why I received over 200 five-star reviews on Google in just nine months!

YOUR BUSINESS CREDIT PROFILE

When you are building business credit, vendors and creditors will use your business credit profile to determine the creditability and lending ability of your business. This profile includes detailed information about your business credit accounts, including utilities, credit cards, banks, suppliers, and other creditors.

This information will include the dates when your accounts were established, any current outstanding balances, any past due accounts, and a detailed history of all your payments. It also provides information available from public records about your business pulled from city, state, county, and federal records, including any potentially negative information about tax liens, lawsuits, judgments, and previous bankruptcy. All of this information informs the lender whether or not your business is credible.

Let's jump straight into understanding your credit profile breakdown.

Make Sure Your Profile is Accurate

It's not uncommon for business owners to find errors in their profiles. Fortunately, the business credit reporting bureaus (the three biggest are Dun & Bradstreet, Equifax, and Experian) are extremely motivated to make sure their data is accurate. Since they sell access to their information to lenders, inaccurate or out-of-date information isn't very valuable!

All three have processes in place to resolve legitimate disputes and correct verifiable errors. What's important to note is that sometimes even minor errors in your profile can make it more difficult for your business to qualify for a loan.

Keep your Personal and Business Credit Separate

This can sometimes be a challenge for business owners, particularly during the early years when business credit is harder to come by. Nevertheless, finding ways to establish business credit and avoiding the use of your personal credit is the best course of action.

For example, instead of using your personal credit cards to purchase supplies or pay for expenses related to your business, apply for a business card. Not only will this help you to establish business credit, but the higher balances that often accompany business expenses can actually hurt your personal credit score because 30 percent of that score is a reflection of how much credit you have, compared to how much credit you use. (This is true even if you pay the balance down to zero at the end of every payment cycle.)

Using your personal credit card does nothing to build a stronger business credit profile, and it will be harder to access business loans down the road. This route also protects you from being personally liable if your business is sued or takes on debt; it will all fall under the business.

Establish Trade Accounts With Your Suppliers

This is one of the best things you can do early in your business to build a strong credit foundation.

Make Sure Your Suppliers Report Your Good Credit Behavior

If your suppliers are not reporting your good history to the bureaus, you may be building a good credit reputation with that particular vendor, but you're not doing anything to build a good credit profile. This is important enough that you should ask every vendor you work if they report to the credit bureaus; you need to seek out those that do.

Use the Credit You Need and Stay Current

The single biggest thing you can do to positively impact your business credit profile is to make regular and timely payments on your business credit accounts. Avoiding the use of credit entirely isn't a good long-term strategy because building a strong profile is about demonstrating that you know how to effectively leverage credit when you need it and that you will make periodic payments on time when you borrow.

WHAT YOU NEED IN PLACE TO START BUILDING A STRONG BUSINESS PROFILE

Business Address

Your business address can make or break your business! ABSOLUTELY DO NOT USE UPS or PO boxes. Get a virtual address instead. When picking a virtual address, STAY AWAY FROM COMPANIES LIKE IPOSTAL as they have 99.9 percent BAD addresses for businesses when it comes to building business credit.

Using these addresses will get your profile FLAGGED really quickly. If you've already set up your business with one of these addresses, there is a way to correct this. You will need to file an amendment with your Secretary of State and the IRS after you get a better location.

If you have an actual physical brick-and-mortar location, this also applies to you. Use your actual physical location and stay away from using your home address (it's public information and doesn't cut it when it comes to getting major funding). Below is a list of companies that you can choose from to obtain a good address. However, please conduct your own research by doing an online search of the address before locking it down, and make sure that it comes up as an office building. THIS IS VERY IMPORTANT!

- Virtual/Corporate Alliance
- Regus
- Opus (reports to the credit bureaus). They will also give you a business phone toll-free number. Click the link in my bio on IG (@hersesecretvault) to go directly to this company.

Business Phone Number

Once you have your address secured, you want to acquire a business toll-free phone number. This will make a difference in being able to operate in different states without having to obtain a foreign entity most of the time. Here are some options: Grasshopper, eVoice, or Opus.

For those of you who use your cell phone number as your business phone number, please know that your cell phone number is not the same as a business phone number. Your business needs to have a separate phone number. And while you may even have a separate local number for your business, it is best when building your business to have a toll-free number because it makes your business seem bigger than it is, giving it a "national presence."

Business Email

Having a professional email shows lenders that they can trust your business. In my professional experience, I have seen that they will oftentimes lend you more money just by having a real business email address. When building business credit, lenders and creditors want to see a real business email such as info@hersecretvault.net or orders@hersecretvault.net. Please DO NOT USE Gmail or Yahoo, etc. Some other options are: GoDaddy, Namecheap, or Google Workspace.

Set Up Your Business Legal Structure

Incorporate your business as a Limited Liability Company (LLC) or a Corporation with the Secretary of State (SOS) office. While there are companies that can do this for you, you can do this yourself by going to your state's SOS website and applying online or in person.

If you want to use a company to do this, I recommend Laughlin Associates who will report your payments to the credit bureaus. (If you decide to explore this option, ask for Wayne

Schoenberger and please tell him Patrice S. Jordan from Her Secret Vault referred you.) His current contact information is:

Local: 775-883-8484
Toll-free: 800-648-0966
Email: wschoenberger@laughlinUSA.com

Get Your Employee Identification Number (EIN)

You can apply for an EIN online at IRS.gov for FREE; however, be aware that there is another site that is copying the IRS and will ask you to pay. If you find yourself at this site asking for a payment, just refresh your browser and apply for your EIN FREE at the official IRS website.

Open a Business Bank Account

Open this right away even if you have no intentions of using it immediately. The older your business bank account is, the better it will be for you when applying for business credit. Some options I suggest are: Navy Federal Credit Union, Wells Fargo, Bank of America, or any credit union.

Establish Your Online Presence

You need an online presence. THIS IS THE MEAT AND POTATOES of your profile! If a lender or vendor can't find you online, they WILL NOT lend to you.

Step 1: Set up a business website

Having a business website is very important to lenders and creditors. They want to see that you are real and have an online presence. This does not need to be a step to stress about. Even if you only have a one-page landing page, that is fine. If you want to build one yourself, some options I recommend are: GoDaddy, Wix, or Squarespace.

Step 2: List your business on ListYourself.net

ListYourself.net is designed to help get your phone number listed in the 411 phone directory assistance. For millions of people, picking up a phone and calling directory assistance remains their preferred way to find and connect with others.

Establish Your Business Credit Profile With the Three Main Business Credit Agencies

1. **D&B**: Largest credit reporting agency. This is where you would generate a "Paydex" score. A score of 80–100 is "low risk" and where you want to be at all times. (Tip: Add three net-30 vendors that report to DNB to acquire a score in 30 days.)

2. **Experian**: Second largest credit monitoring agency that's used by credit card companies to determine your approval. Make sure your business score is 76–100 before applying for credit cards.

3. **Equifax Commercial**: Third largest credit reporting agency. Most lenders pull from here when making lending decisions.

Monitor Your Business Credit Profiles

You can also monitor your business credit profile with all three of the main business credit agencies via Nav.com. However, please remember that Nav pulls from all three of the agencies and ONLY monitors your scores. This is not where your scores are generated.

One of the most powerful benefits of using Nav is that it can also be used as a tradeline (this is discussed more in chapter 4). Use the following link to get a discount on Nav: https://bit.ly/37qBuVh.

2

DIFFERENT TYPES OF LEGAL STRUCTURES FOR YOUR BUSINESS

I n this chapter I am going to go through some of the most commonly used business structures. Some of them you may be familiar with and others you may not be! When setting up your business structure, it is important to take into consideration several different factors, such as the risk level of your business, your business goals and objectives, and also your personal goals and objectives.

I also strongly advise that you get professional advice to ensure that your business is legally structured in a way that is most appropriate for your circumstances.

Sole Proprietorship

A sole proprietorship is easy to form and gives you complete control of your business. You're automatically considered to be a sole proprietor if you perform business activities but don't register as any other kind of business. Sole proprietorships do not produce a separate business entity. This means your business assets and liabilities are not separate from your personal assets and liabilities, and you can be held personally liable for the debts and obligations of the business.

If you operate as a sole proprietor, you are still able to get a trade name, but it can also be harder to raise money because you can't sell stock, and banks are hesitant to lend to sole proprietorships.

Operating as a sole proprietor can be a good choice for low-risk businesses and owners who want to test their business idea before forming a more formal business.

Partnerships

Partnerships are the simplest structure for two or more people to own a business together. There are two common kinds of partnerships: limited partnership (LP) and limited liability partnership (LLP). Limited partnerships have only one general partner with unlimited liability, and all other partners have limited liability.

The partners with limited liability also tend to have limited control over the company, which is documented in a partnership agreement. Profits are passed through to personal tax returns, and the general partner—the partner without limited liability—must also pay self-employment taxes. LLP partnerships are like limited partnerships but give limited liability to every owner. An LLP protects each partner from debts against the partnership, meaning they won't be responsible for the actions of other partners.

Partnerships can be a good choice for businesses with multiple owners, professional groups (like attorneys), and other groups that want to test their business idea before forming a more formal business.

Limited Liability Company (LLC)

An LLC is a form of business that lets you take advantage of the benefits of both the corporation and partnership business structures.

LLCs protect you from personal liability. In most instances, your personal assets, such as your vehicle, house, and savings accounts, won't be at risk in case your LLC faces bankruptcy or lawsuits. Profits and losses can get passed through to your personal income without facing corporate taxes. However, members of an LLC are considered self-employed and must pay self-employment tax contributions toward Medicare and Social Security. LLCs can have a limited life in many states.

When a member joins or leaves an LLC, some states may require the LLC to be dissolved and re-formed with new membership—unless there's already an agreement in place within the LLC for buying, selling, and transferring ownership.

LLCs can be a good choice for medium- or higher-risk businesses, owners who have significant personal assets they want to be protected, and owners who want to pay a lower tax rate than they would with a corporation.

C Corporation (C Corp)

A C corporation, sometimes called a C corp, is a legal entity that's separate from its owners. Corporations can make a profit, can be taxed, and can be held legally liable.

Corporations offer the strongest protection to their owners from personal liability, but the cost to form a corporation is higher than other structures. Corporations also require more extensive record keeping, operational processes, and reporting.

Unlike sole proprietors, partnerships, and LLCs, corporations pay income tax on their profits. In some cases, corporate profits are taxed twice: first, when the company makes a profit, and again when dividends are paid to shareholders on their personal tax returns.

Corporations have a completely independent life separate from their shareholders. If a shareholder leaves the company or sells his or her shares, the C corp can continue doing business relatively undisturbed.

Corporations have an advantage when it comes to raising capital because they can raise funds through the sale of stock, which can also be a benefit in attracting employees. Corporations can be a good choice for medium- or higher-risk businesses, businesses that need to raise money, and businesses that plan to "go public" or eventually be sold.

S Corp

An S corporation, sometimes called an S corp, is a special type of corporation that's designed to avoid the double taxation drawback of regular C corps. S corps allow profits, and some losses, to be passed through directly to owners' personal income without ever being subject to corporate tax rates.

Not all states tax S corps equally, but most recognize them the same way the federal government does and taxes the shareholders accordingly. Some states tax S corps on profits above a specified limit, and other states don't recognize the S corp election at all, simply treating the business as a C corp. S corps must file with the IRS to get S corp status, a different process from registering with their state.

There are special limits on S corps. S corps can't have more than 100 shareholders, and all shareholders must be U.S. citizens. If you operate as an S corp, you'll still have to follow the strict filing and operational processes of a C corp. S corps also have an independent life, just like C corps. If a shareholder leaves the company or sells his or her shares, the S corp can continue doing business relatively undisturbed.

S corps can be a good choice for businesses that would otherwise be a C corp but meet the criteria to file as an S corp.

B Corps

A benefit corporation, sometimes called a B corp, is a for-profit corporation recognized by a majority of U.S. states. B corps are different from C corps in purpose, accountability, and transparency but aren't different in how they're taxed. B corps are driven by both mission and profit. Shareholders hold the company accountable to produce some sort of public benefit in addition to a financial profit.

Some states require B corps to submit annual benefit reports that demonstrate their contribution to the public good. There are several third-party B corp certification services, but none are required for a company to be legally considered a B corp in a state where the legal status is available.

Close Corporation

Close corporations resemble B corps but have a less traditional corporate structure. These shed many formalities that typically govern corporations and apply to smaller companies. State rules vary, but shares are usually barred from public trading. Close corporations can be run by a small group of shareholders without a board of directors.

Nonprofit Corporation

Nonprofit corporations are organized to do charity, education, religious, literary, or scientific work. Because their work benefits the public, nonprofits can receive tax-exempt status, meaning they don't pay state or federal taxes or income taxes on any profits they make. Nonprofits must file with the IRS to get tax exemption, a different process from registering with their state. Nonprofit corporations need to follow organizational rules very similar to a regular C corp. They also need to follow special rules about what they do with any profits they earn. For example, they can't distribute profits to members or political campaigns.

Nonprofits are often called 501(c)(3) corporations—a reference to the section of the Internal Revenue Code that is most commonly used to grant tax-exempt status.

Cooperative

A cooperative is a business or organization owned by and operated for the benefit of those using its services. Profits and earnings generated by the cooperative are distributed among the members, also known as user-owners.

Typically, an elected board of directors and officers runs the cooperative while regular members have voting power to control the direction of the cooperative. Members can become part of the cooperative by purchasing shares, though the number of shares they hold does not affect the weight of their vote.

COMBINING DIFFERENT BUSINESS STRUCTURES

Designations like S corp and nonprofit aren't strictly business structures—they can also be understood as a tax status. It's possible for an LLC to be taxed as a C corp, an S corp, or a nonprofit. These arrangements are far less common and can be more difficult to set up.

If you're considering one of these non-standard structures, you should speak with a business counselor or an attorney to help you decide which structure and tax status is most appropriate for you and your business.

3

WHAT EIN-ONLY BUSINESS CREDIT REALLY IS

In this chapter I want to take a moment to explain to you what EIN-only business credit really means. EIN-only business credit is the ability for a/your business to operate/ stand alone on its own. Think of EIN-only business credit the same way you would think about you having a social security number. As an individual person, you are identified by the government, credit bureaus, and many others by your social security number.

In order for you to purchase a house, buy a car, get a cell phone, buy land, etc., you need to have good personal credit. Your social security number and you are one person.

With your business, it is no different. You need to build a strong business credit profile in stages for your business to be able to stand alone by itself so that you don't have to act as a personal guarantor for your business.

To do this, you will need to build business credit from tier 1 through tier 5 without skipping steps. Doing this will give your business the ability to build a strong foundation for itself and therefore put it in a position to stand alone without attaching your personal social security number (unless it's for identification purposes only).

Before we move on to the next chapter, I want you to be very clear about what this means. Before providing your social security number to ANY vendor, make sure they are just trying to confirm that you are a real person and they are not "PGing" (personal guaranteeing) you.

Just to be safe, I suggest that you lock all of your personal credit accounts with the three major credit bureaus. This can be done by calling them or notifying them online.

4

BUILDING BUSINESS
CREDIT (EIN ONLY)

As we just discussed in chapter 3, when it comes to building business credit without using your social security number as a personal guarantee, you have to create a profile where the business can stand alone. To accomplish this, you need to look at the five associated tiers. When you consider these tiers, think of MAJOR vendors, i.e., vendors that are everywhere.

While you are building your business credit profile, do not apply for major vendors out of the proper tier. While building, I want you to focus not on just what you get approved for but how much.

When you apply in the correct tier, your approval amounts will be MUCH higher. You should expect nothing under $10K per approval. Now we get to work! As you read this chapter, I want you to keep two things in mind:

1. FOLLOW EACH STEP **IN ORDER.** DO NOT SKIP ANY STEPS, PLEASE.
2. RUN YOUR OWN RACE AND STAY FOCUSED ON YOUR BUSINESS PROFILE!

BUILDING TIER 1: NET-30/Subscription Vendors

Opening accounts with net-30/subscription vendors will help you get started with building tier 1 business credit. Below is a list of vendors that can help you establish your business credit. You need to use these vendors until they report. If done right, they can report within forty-five to sixty days or less. When it comes to the net-30 vendors accounts, DO NOT PAY ON THE EXACT DATE THAT YOUR INVOICES ARE DUE. Pay about two weeks after your purchase to acquire a higher Paydex score! For the subscription-based vendors, you keep them until they report to the Business bureau. Then you can stop your subscription. And, no, they won't take your score away from you. The goal here is to apply and get approved for these credit accounts. Make sure you have at least three vendors that reports to DNB to gain a Paydex score I always recommend getting four to five accounts right away, as out of the five, three will report faster (rather than only getting three and waiting). Here are my recommendations: Quill; Grainger; Uline; Nav ($39.99); eCredable ($19.99) Fairfigure card

Order from Grainger, Uline, and Quill between $100 and $200 per month. The more you spend, the better your results. Order on Thursdays and then pay your invoices the second or third Monday after your purchase. This shows the vendors that you're responsible.

Nav.com tracks your business profile and has every type of business service you will need as a business owner. A great benefit of enrolling with Nav is that if you upgrade your Nav account to the credit builder ($39.99 or higher at the time of this publication), it will report your monthly payment to all three credit agencies. In other words, this will be adding a new tradeline to your profile, which I highly recommend.

Keep in mind that NAV stands for the net asset value of your company, nothing more nothing less. After the tradeline reports, you can stop paying for it. Once you stop paying, you will then see a letter score, not a number. PLEASE don't freak out. Nav is only a tradeline. The bureaus are the ones that generate your credit score; Nav merely monitors it.

Credit ratings are normally expressed in letters such as "A" or "B". A and B letters are good. Just a quick FYI on your Nav profile: You may see a low Equifax score—no worries—Equifax comes in play more around tier 3, and by the time you get to tier 3, you would see a better Equifax score. Equifax is always the last score to go up as there are only certain vendors that only report to them.

eCredable Lift offers a way to potentially improve your credit score by reporting your utility, cell phone, and internet payment history to credit bureaus. Here are the key features and benefits of the service:

1. Utility and Telecom Payments Reporting: By reporting up to twenty-four months of your utility, cell phone, and internet payment history, eCredable Lift can help you build or improve your credit profile. This can be particularly beneficial if you have a limited credit history or are trying to rebuild your credit.

2. Improved Credit Opportunities: With an improved credit score, you may qualify for better credit cards and personal loans, potentially saving money through lower interest rates and better terms.

3. Monthly Credit Score Updates: eCredable Lift provides monthly updates of your VantageScore 3.0 credit score, allowing you to monitor your progress and see the impact of the reported payments over time.

This service can be especially useful for individuals who have a thin credit file or no traditional credit history, enabling them to leverage their consistent payment habits to build a stronger credit profile.

FairFigure Business Credit: Boost your business credit & growth with up to 60% improvement in 3 months + same-day funding access with the FairFigure Capital Card. FairFigure is your credit co-pilot from startup to enterprise. Firefigure offers:

1. Business Credit Monitoring services
   See what lenders see! Track your business credit health, uncover hidden issues, and build a score for better funding options

2. EIN only Business Credit Card
   Build your business credit AND get funded at the same time! No personal guarantees, paperwork, or FICO required. Funding is based on business revenue, not personal credit scores.

3. Business Funding
   Get the recognition you deserve for your on time payments. Your dedicated funding advisor will fast track you to additional funding offers.

   - Reports to business credit bureaus
   - No deposit required
   - No personal guarantee or personal credit checks
   - Select your own payback terms
   - Best in class monitoring + 2 tradelines

FairFigure Premium monitor is the perfect tool for your business. Get access to your Foundation Report which is your compass to your business credit and commercial scores. On time payments are reported to the bureaus boosting your scores and potentially qualifying you for new capital. We also include $1,000,000 in Identity Theft P

BUILDING TIER 3: FLEET CREDIT TIER

All six combined vendors from tier 1 and tier 2 need to be reporting before moving onto this tier. Also, remember that when you apply for a business fleet, do not put your social security number on the application unless it specifically says for identification purpose only. If not, leave it blank!

Here are my recommendations: Shell; BP Master Card; Chevron.

BUILDING TIER 4: MAJOR CREDIT CARD

Make sure your Experian score is between 75 and 100 before applying for credit cards. And, remember, when applying for business credit cards, do not put your social security number on the application. Leave it blank. This will force the company to pull your business credit.

Now, when applying, if you get a message saying that your EIN and social security number can't be the same, call the vendor instead and apply online, letting them know you don't want to personally guarantee "PG" this application: Sam's Club Master Card; Amazon Net 55; Wells Fargo; Capital One.

BUILDING TIER 5: BUSINESS LOANS

When you get to this stage, congratulate yourself! You have entered the BIG, BIG LEAGUES now! Now, before getting funding in this tier, your Equifax score needs to be strong.

IMPORTANCE OF BUILDING TIERS IN ORDER

You already know by now: Do not apply for major vendors out of the proper tier because it's not what you get approved for but how much. And by applying in the correct tier, your approval amounts will be MUCH higher (nothing under $10K per approval). But before we wrap up and move on, I want to dive in a little deeper here. The tier 1 to tier 5 vendors listed in this chapter are considered major players in the business credit industry, but there are other vendors that you can apply for without skipping the major steps without getting declined.

What follows is a better explanation:

BP gas (major) tier 3; Arco gas (not major); you can apply in tier 1.

Staples (major) tier 2: Business T-Shirt Club (not major) tier 1.

Capital One (major) tier 4; BILL Spend & Expense (not major) tier 1 (with income to show).

Note: If you run into any issues with acquiring your tier 1 vendors here is a script below to help you.

Calling Vendors *(this script works better with Quill):*

Once a representative answers, they are going to introduce themselves and then ask you for your name.

You: Hello, my name is _____. I would like to speak to an account manager/supervisor please.

(The representative is going to seem kind of confused when you ask for an account manager and will then start to ask you questions.)

You: Make it seem like you're very disappointed with their customer service from the other representatives. Tell the representative that you were placed on hold for about thirty minutes and that the phone/representative then hung up on you before coming back to the phone to address your issues fully. The representative will apologize and try to help.

You will then let the representative know you were advised that if you placed an order, your account would be a net 30. Tell them you are disappointed that the previous representative lied to you and then hung up on you.

The representative will then place you on hold and try to contact their supervisor. If they don't place you on hold, they probably will try to help you themselves.

If the representative comes back and says that you have to place an order, you have to stick to the script and say, "I need an account manager. This is unacceptable." Then say, "If (I/ YOU) knew this in advance, I/YOU would have never opened this account with this company. I/YOU are not responsible for the misinformation provided by your team member who is supposed to be trained and knowledgeable in customer service (and might I add was very rude)."

The representative will then say you have to, at least, place an order.

Option 1: If you placed an order before, advise the representative that you placed an order and the account is still not a net 30. Then use that against the representative by saying, "You are telling me the same thing, but, as you can see, my account is not a net 30." At that point, the representative should have someone update your account to net 30.

Option 2: Advise the representative that you have an existing order sitting in your cart. Tell them, "I don't mind submitting that order as long as my account will be marked as net 30." (Have $100 worth of items in your cart.)

Option 3: If the representative starts to piss you off, hang up and take a deep breath. Call them again and inform them that you were hung up on (LOL!).

The reason for net 30 and going so hard is you can buy now and pay later, which is a win-win!

You can find on YouTube a training video for those of you who learn better by watching video steps: https://www.youtube.com/watch?v=gk4QGLEnjjM

5

FINTECH CREDIT CARDS

Fintech, short for financial technology, refers to financial tech companies. Fintech cards are a great option for you to utilize when you need a business credit card in the beginning stages of your business and you are not yet at the point where you are ready to apply for tier 4 credit cards. Essentially, Fintech credit cards can help you build your business credit while you are still in the early phases.

In the credit card world, these cards, which are issued by financial tech companies (as compared to a major bank credit card in tier 4) do not look at anything to evaluate your businesses creditworthiness other than your bank's financials for the last three months. Then they extend to you a business credit card if you qualify for it. It is always best to make sure your business bank account is three months or older and you have $5k minimum coming into the account consistently for the last three months.

BILL Spend & Expense: a spend and expense management platform for businesses with the added benefit of a business credit card. The company provides funds for small businesses as well as tools to manage spending and budgets.

Capital on Tap: the credit card built for small businesses. · No annual fee · Get $200 back if you spend $15,000 in your first three months · Unlimited free 1.5% cashback · Great rates.

Ramp: a fintech company that developed a corporate card designed to help businesses spend less, reached a unicorn status valuation of $1.6 billion after raising $115 million in Secured Business funding.

Torpago business credit card: the corporate card and expense management platform designed for modern business. They combine the power of their cards and software so your business can control spending and empower your team.

Charity (great for those of you with nonprofits): the credit card program for your nonprofit, with no annual fee, backed by Mastercard Zero Liability and ID Theft Protection. It builds organizational credit history.

Clearbanc: low-cost cash advances for e-commerce corporations and LLCs. Bottom line: this lender specializes in financing online and tech companies in the startup phase, with relatively low fees compared to similar options. But you'll need to be registered as an LLC or corporation to qualify.

Hatch: a digital-first bank improving how people save, spend, borrow, and send money by creating strategic relationships with fintech companies.

Here's a list of other credit card options:

- BP Mastercard
- Brex
- Hatch
- FairFigure
- Floor & Decor
- Jeeves
- KleerCard
- Revenue
- Rho
- Sam's Club
- TomoCredit

6

CORPORATE LEASING

Corporate leasing means acquiring a lease for one or more residential units under which one entity will rent all such units from the borrower and will have the right to sublease such units to individual subtenants. In other words, corporate leasing is the term used for getting properties under your business. If you are looking to acquire properties for short-term rentals (such as Airbnb), you want to make sure to ask the property management company or leasing office if they offer corporate leasing.

Now, Airbnb is not the only option. If you choose not to use your corporate leases for Airbnb purposes, you can also acquire corporate leasing under the business for yourself or staff to reside in.

Some leasing offices will ask for a background check on anyone living there, and I usually pass on those as it's not 100 percent a real corporate lease because when you acquire a corporate leasing it should be off of the strength of the business only, and not the people staying there.

However, if you do choose to do this, it is of course your choice, but keep in mind this can hold you liable for anything that may happen with the business as they now have access to your social security number and other personal information.

AIRBNB CORPORATE LEASING

What is Airbnb? Airbnb, Inc. operates an online marketplace for lodging, primarily homestays for vacation rentals, and tourism activities. It is based in San Francisco, California. The platform is accessible via the web and through their mobile app. When it comes to Airbnb, you must do your due diligence. There are a few restricted states; however, restricted doesn't mean impossible; you just have to follow your state guidelines and always stay away from HOA communities in restricted states.

Nevada, Florida, and California are considered restricted states, but they are also some of the top-earning states for Airbnb. So you see, restricted definitely does not mean impossible! If you reside in one of these states (Nevada, Florida, or California), please be sure to check your local guidelines before starting an Airbnb.

The information on this page and the following only applies to Las Vegas, Nevada, restrictions. Please keep in mind that while there may be restrictions in the state where you live or want to operate in, you can still operate as long as you follow state guidelines.

It's important for you to understand your local laws if you want to become an Airbnb host. They provide a platform and marketplace, but they don't provide legal advice.

Even so, they do share information to help you understand laws and other rules that relate to short-term rentals in various cities. The information they share is not exhaustive, but it should help you start your research on local laws.

Las Vegas, Nevada, Guidelines

If you have questions, you can check the City of Las Vegas Short-Term Rental Licensing page, contact the Las Vegas Planning and Zoning Department, or another local authority, such as a local lawyer or tax professional.

Building and Housing Standards

The building and construction codes (Title 16 of the Las Vegas Municipal Code) specify minimum construction, design, and maintenance standards for buildings, including regulations on habitability, health, and safety. Certain regulations which are applicable to residential and non-residential uses may be relevant to your listing. You should consult these codes to see if your listing implicates any of their requirements, or contact the building and safety department directly.

License Requirements

You need a license to offer a short-term rental to guests in Las Vegas. Check the Las Vegas Short-Term Rentals page for more information.

Short-Term Rental licenses

As of December 5, 2018, the City of Las Vegas limited short-term rentals to owner-occupied properties and hosts who were already licensed or had a pending application at the time, along with certain requirements. Check Las Vegas' short-term rental licensing information and instructions for up-to-date information.

Operational Requirements

Las Vegas requires short-term rental hosts to follow a number of operational requirements. Check the Las Vegas Short-Term Rentals page for more information about insurance, zoning, safety, taxes, and more.

Insurance

Hosts who apply for a business license are required to provide proof of liability insurance coverage with a $500,000 minimum amount.

Zoning Restrictions

Zoning restrictions include a 660-foot density limit between short-term rentals for all single-family and multi-family homes. For example, short-term rentals may only be used for dwelling, lodging, or overnight accommodations.

Other commercial events that are typically held at banquet facilities, such as weddings, parties, and receptions, are prohibited at short-term rentals.

Safety

The city conducts property inspections of short-term rental properties as part of the Conditional Use Verification (CUV) Permit approval process. The inspector will verify the number of bedrooms in the house and will check for safety requirement compliance.

Check the short-term rental application instructions for more information about the inspection process, including a detailed list. All operators of short-term rentals must make payment of applicable room taxes. Contact the Las Vegas License Office for more information.

Other Contracts and Rules

As a host, you need to understand and abide by other contracts or rules that bind you, including leases, co-op rules, HOA rules, or other rules established by tenant organizations.

You should be able to find out more by contacting your housing authority (such as a community council) or landlord. Your lease (or another contract) might also have specific details. If you're not in any of these restricted areas, you are free to operate your Airbnb; however, I highly suggest doing some research in your state before starting. Airbnb also provides many articles on restrictions and how to stay up to code in your state.

THINGS YOU NEED TO START A CORPORATE LEASE

The paperwork for obtaining an apartment or a house is much different. I will explain the differences here.

House Rentals

To secure a corporate lease for a house, a landlord may do a background check on you and require one month of your bank statement; however, it all depends on the listing and the landlord.

I generally highly recommended staying away from listings with these types of requirements; however, if you want to be a little daring and go for it, then have the landlord run a background check on your cleaning company. The reason for this is, since they will be coming in and out, they don't need to know they are your cleaners—they are employees who work for you!

If you use this tip, you will not only keep your own personal social security number off records, but you will also get a free background check on your cleaners (two birds with one stone)!

Apartment Rentals

When it comes to apartments, the requirements to secure a corporate lease are usually not as intense as the requirements for a house. This is because most apartments do corporate leasing so they are already familiar with the application process and they have pre-established processes and requirements.

However, not all requirements are the same with all apartments; they may still require you to provide some combination of your business license, tax ID, taxes schedule C, and/or your business financial statements.

Apartments usually ask for one or the other, so choose what works for you. I typically go after units that only ask for EIN or business license (i.e., Secretary of State paperwork). If you have the income to show for your business, then feel free to choose one of the other options.

OTHER INCOME-GENERATING OPPORTUNITIES FOR YOUR CORPORATE LEASE

Outside of Airbnb, you can create other income opportunities for your properties like making it into a Content Studio /

Theme. Unlike Airbnb, these options are great because no one is spending the night and you can make more money with less work. Keep in mind that this is golden, as most locations ask you for the list of everyone spending the night so they can run a background check, and this option will eliminate that problem. Below you'll find a list of places you can list your unit if you turn it into a content studio:

Peerspace; Airbnb; your website (put in your bio); connect with photographers and offer your location; Image Locations (selected states); Location Resource; Giggster.com; Pure locations; 1st option.

7

HOW TO AQUIRE YOUR FIRST APARTMENT/HOUSE

RESEARCH STUDY

U tilize the list of residential property websites to find systems. When trying to find a residence, you can additionally do something called driving for leases. This is where you canvass the areas for a lease indication by exclusive proprietors (NOT HOME MANAGEMENT COMPANIES). These indicators will offer a call number for the owner. Real estate professionals have, likewise, been searching for brand-new buildings.

- PADMAPPER.COM
- REALTOR.COM
- RENTALADS.COM
- RENTALS.COM

- RENTBITS.COM
- RENT.COM
- JUNGLE.COM
- RENTLER.COM
- SHOWMETHERENT.COM
- TRULIA.COM
- ULOOP.COM
- WALKSCORE.COM
- ZILLOW.COM
- ZUMPER.COM
- RENT.COM
- FACEBOOK MARKETPLACE
- ONRADPAD.COM
- CRAIGLIST

Solid marketing research is necessary to assist you in determining the very best cities for Airbnb rental. There are a number of ways of obtaining data when seeking short-term rentals.

- The Airbnb website itself can offer a lot of details concerning your target market.
- You will recognize which markets have a demand for details, enhancing designs, distance, facilities, number of bedrooms, and residential or commercial property kinds.
- Another method of discovering an Airbnb property is to look for tourist attractions and locations creating a buzz in the city. This could be clubs, shopping centers,

parks, or coastlines. Such details can be located through traveling sites and also online evaluations.

Should You Mention the Airbnb?

- No. Generally, if you are inquiring about an apartment, it is not required to mention Airbnb. Airbnb is a market tool and not your business model. The word Airbnb alone scares property managers.

Do You Need a Business License?

- Yes and no. At some locations you will need an LLC to acquire a corporate lease. At other locations you can use EIN only; however, it's best to have a full business up and running.

Should you Sign the Lease in Your Own Name?

- NEVERRRRRRRR!! This is strictly business-related. Ensure you sign the lease using only your company name. Signing with your personal name could lead to termination of the lease and may also affect any sub-leasing arrangements if you reside on the property. The apartment management company can even sue for eviction and add it to your personal credit.

Can You Charge Higher Rates Than Hotels Charging Nearby?

- No. Your Airbnb properties must cost the guests much less than the charge taken by hotels.

Do You Have to Create a New Business?

- No. Feel free to use your existing business. I currently have a business credit company that was established in 2014. I use the document from this company to establish corporate leases. @hersecretvault

Picking a location

When picking a location:
- It's best to be near shops and restaurants.
- It's best to have something on the ground floor.
- It's best to have one or two bedrooms.
- It's best to rent, NOT buy a property.
- Get a unit that's cost effective until you start making money.

Systems

Air bna.co System: "See how much units around you charge."
Zoho: "Keeps track of properties you rent from and all messages."
YourPorter: "Keep your Airbnbs organized."

Notes:

- Have about five Airbnb accounts. WHY? In case one gets shut down.
- Have service people on standby.
- Where to shop: UTILIZE your business credit.

Where to list your properties

- Airbnb
- Furnished Finder (Travel nurse)
- Bookings.com
- Smartertravel.com
- Hellolanding
- Traveladvisor.com
- Expedia.com
- Theculturetrip.com
- Trip 101
- Travelnursehousing.com
- Apartments.com
- Zillow
- Apartment Finders
- Avail
- Craigslist
- Facebook marketplace
- People with pets
- Apartment List
- Zumper
- Padmapper

Note: Some of these may not be available in your state. Simply type in: Airbnb (yourstatename) and find more listing areas that work for your Airbnb state.

BONUS: Did you know that flight attendants stay in something called a crash pad when they travel?

What is a crash pad? A crash pad is a place where traveling professionals stay when they are in town. Most attendants work two weeks on and two weeks off when they are working in a state outside of their own. They will need a place to stay, and some even get relocated to another state and have to find temporary housing when they travel. Usually, a crash pad has about four bunk beds in each room. And, typically, the host charges $400 per month per bed (moneymaker).

Start talking to flight attendants when you travel, and give them your card. Most of the time they will keep your house booked.

8

FURNISHING YOUR AIRBNB IN FORTY-EIGHT TO SEVENTY-TWO HOURS

Setting up an Airbnb quickly and efficiently can be a daunting task, but with the right strategy and resources, it's entirely possible to furnish your property within forty-eight to seventy-two hours. This chapter will guide you through various vendors and options to achieve this, focusing on the speed and convenience they offer. We'll also dive into the details of Amazon Pay by Invoice, a flexible payment option that can help streamline your purchasing process.

1. Understanding the Timeline

When aiming to furnish an Airbnb in such a short timeframe, planning is crucial. Here's a step-by-step approach:

1. List Your Needs: Determine the essential items required for your Airbnb (e.g., beds, sofas, dining tables, kitchenware).
2. Budgeting: Establish your budget to avoid overspending and to ensure you allocate funds effectively.
3. Vendor Selection: Choose vendors that offer quick delivery and a wide range of products.
4. Payment Methods: Consider payment options that provide flexibility and ease of transaction.

2. Key Vendors for Quick Furnishing

Here are some top vendors known for their efficiency and variety, making them ideal for furnishing your Airbnb quickly:

1. Letgo and Facebook Marketplace: These platforms are great for finding second-hand furniture locally. They allow for quick pickups and often have negotiable prices.
2. Wayfair Business: Wayfair offers a business program with perks such as fast shipping and bulk purchase discounts. Their extensive catalog covers all furniture and décor needs.
3. Target: Known for its broad range of affordable home goods, Target is perfect for finding essential items. They also offer same-day delivery in many locations.
4. Floor & Decor: Specializing in flooring and tile, Floor & Decor provides high-quality materials that can be acquired swiftly to give your Airbnb a polished look.

5. Thrift Shops: Local thrift shops can be gold mines for unique and budget-friendly furniture. While selection varies, these shops often have hidden gems that can add character to your space.

6. Amazon: Amazon is unparalleled in its selection and delivery speed. With the right planning, you can get almost everything you need within two days.

3. Spotlight on Amazon Pay by Invoice

Amazon Pay by Invoice is a convenient payment option for those looking to manage their cash flow effectively while furnishing their Airbnb. Here's a detailed look at what it offers:

Not a Business Credit: Unlike traditional business credit, Amazon Pay by Invoice is available to anyone. It doesn't require a lengthy application process.

Flexible Payment Terms: This option allows you to purchase items and pay the invoice within 30 days, providing a grace period to manage your finances.

Large Inventory Access: With Amazon's vast product range, you can find virtually everything you need, from furniture to kitchen essentials, all in one place.

Speedy Delivery: Prime members can benefit from same-day, one-day, or two-day shipping on many items, ensuring you get your purchases quickly.

Ease of Use: The process is straightforward—add items to your cart, select Pay by Invoice at checkout, and complete your order. You'll receive an invoice to be paid within the agreed timeframe.

4. Combining Resources for Efficiency

Using a mix of these vendors can help you maximize both time and budget. Here's how you can strategically combine them:

Immediate Essentials: Use Amazon for immediate essentials like kitchenware, linens, and small furniture pieces.

Large Furniture: Order from Wayfair Business or Target for larger items like beds and sofas, taking advantage of their fast shipping options.

Local Pickups: Supplement with local purchases from Letgo, Facebook Marketplace, and thrift shops to fill in gaps and add unique touches.

Flooring & Decor: Use Floor & Decor for any necessary upgrades to flooring or tiling to enhance the overall look of your Airbnb.

5. Final Tips

Preparation: Before you start shopping, have a clear plan and measurements of your space to avoid purchasing items that won't fit.

Bulk Purchases: Consider buying in bulk where possible to save on costs and ensure consistency in your Airbnb's design.

Assembly: Factor in the time for assembly. If you're short on time, consider hiring a local handyman or using furniture assembly services.

By leveraging these vendors and the flexibility of Amazon Pay by Invoice, you can efficiently and effectively furnish your Airbnb in forty-eight to seventy-two hours, ensuring your property is guest-ready in no time.

9

LET'S WORK ON YOUR PITCH

Creating a compelling pitch is essential when negotiating with property managers or landlords. A well-crafted sales call can make the difference between securing a property and missing out. This chapter will guide you through the process of developing and delivering an effective pitch to property managers, ensuring that you build strong connections and present a compelling case for your Airbnb business.

1. Preparing Your Pitch

Before you initiate any conversation, it's crucial to be well prepared. Here are some key steps:

Research the Property: Understand the specifics of the property you're interested in and the local rental market.

Know Your Needs: Be clear about what you require from the property and what you can offer in return.

Develop Key Points: Outline the main points you want to convey during your pitch.

2. Building a Connection

Developing a genuine connection with the property manager or landlord is the first step:

Personal Introduction: Start by introducing yourself and explaining your background and experience in managing Airbnb properties.

Express Care: Reassure them that their property will be well maintained and respected.

3. Presenting with Confidence

When presenting your pitch, confidence is key:

Be Upfront and Straightforward: Clearly state your intentions and how you plan to use the property.

Highlight Benefits: Emphasize how your management will benefit the property owner, such as reliable income and property upkeep.

4. Handling Inquiries and Negotiating

Be prepared for questions and be ready to negotiate:

Solid Bargaining Position: Know your limits and be prepared to negotiate terms that work for both parties.

Answer Questions: Be ready to provide detailed answers about how you manage properties, handle guests, and ensure property care.

5. Building a Relationship

A successful pitch often leads to a long-term relationship:

Start a Conversation: Engage in a friendly conversation to build rapport.

Establish Trust: Show genuine interest in the property owner's needs and concerns.

6. Reducing Perceived Risks

Position your proposal as a low-risk opportunity for the property owner:

Experimentation: Present the idea of re-renting as a trial or experiment rather than a permanent change. This can make the property owner feel more comfortable and less pressured.

Offer Incentives: Consider offering something in return to sweeten the deal, such as a higher rent amount or a longer lease period.

7. Making an Attractive Offer

Strengthen your pitch with attractive offers:

Revenue Sharing: Propose a deal where the property owner shares in the revenue generated from Airbnb rentals.

Longer Lease Commitment: Show your commitment by offering to sign a longer lease, which provides stability and assurance to the property owner.

Multiple Units: If applicable, offer to rent multiple units or properties, which can be more appealing to property managers.

Advance Payments: Offering to prepay rent can demonstrate your financial stability and commitment.

Sample Pitch Outline

Introduction:

Dear [Apartment Complex Manager's Name],

I hope this message finds you well. My name is [Your Name], and I am interested in learning more about the corporate leasing options at [Apartment Complex Name].

Could you please provide information on whether you offer corporate leases and the terms and conditions associated with them? We are looking for a reliable and comfortable housing solution in the [City/Area] for our corporate needs.

Here are a few details about our requirements:

- **Lease Term**: [Duration, e.g., 6 months, 1 year, etc.]
- **Number of Units**: [Number of units needed]
- **Move-in Date**: [Preferred move-in date]

We would appreciate any details you can share regarding availability, pricing, and the application process. Additionally, if there are any special requirements or documentation needed for corporate leases, please let us know.

Thank you for your time and assistance. We look forward to the possibility of partnering with [Apartment Complex Name] for our corporate housing needs.

Best regards,

[Your Name]
[Your Phone Number]
[Your Email Address]

Inquiry for Corporate Leasing from Homeowner

Subject: Corporate Leasing Opportunity Inquiry

Dear [Homeowner's Name],

I hope this email finds you well. My name is [Your Name], and I am reaching out to inquire about the possibility of leasing your property located at [Property Address] for corporate housing purposes.

We are seeking a property that can provide a comfortable and reliable housing solution for our corporate needs. Could you please let us know if you are open to corporate leases and, if so, provide details about the terms and conditions?

Here are some details about our requirements:

- **Lease Term:** [Duration, e.g., 6 months, 1 year, etc.]
- **Number of Occupants:** [Number of occupants]
- **Move-in Date:** [Preferred move-in date]

We are committed to maintaining the property in excellent condition and ensuring timely rent payments. Please let us know if you are interested and if we can schedule a time to discuss further.

Thank you for your consideration.

Best regards,
[Your Name]
[Your Phone Number]
[Your Email Address]

Follow-Up Email for Corporate Leasing Inquiry

Subject: Follow-Up on Corporate Leasing Inquiry

Dear [Recipient's Name],

I hope this email finds you well. I am writing to follow up on my previous inquiry regarding the possibility of corporate leasing at [Apartment Complex Name] / your property located at [Property Address].

As mentioned, we are very interested in exploring corporate leasing options and would appreciate any information you can provide regarding availability, pricing, and the application process. We are keen to discuss how we can move forward and potentially arrange a visit to the property.

Please let me know if you need any additional information from our side or if there is a convenient time for us to discuss this further.

Thank you once again for your time and consideration.

Best regards,
[Your Name]
[Your Phone Number]
[Your Email Address]

10

HOW TO MAKE YOUR AIRBNB STAND OUT

In a crowded market, making your Airbnb stand out is essential to attract guests and ensure they have a memorable stay. This chapter provides actionable tips to elevate your property, making it a top choice for travelers. From hiring a skilled photographer to creating a unique theme, these strategies will help you transform your Airbnb into an irresistible destination.

1. Hire a Dope Photographer

High-quality photos are crucial for making a great first impression. Here's why you should invest in a professional photographer:

First Impressions: Professional photos highlight your property's best features, making it more appealing to potential guests.

Higher Bookings: Listings with high-quality images tend to receive more bookings and can command higher rates.

Stand Out: In a sea of listings, professional photos help your property stand out, making it more likely to be noticed and selected.

2. Add as Many Amenities as Possible

Amenities can significantly enhance your guests' experience. Here are some must-haves:

Basic Amenities: Ensure essentials like Wi-Fi, heating, air conditioning, and kitchen appliances are available.

Comfort Enhancers: Add extra touches like plush towels, high-quality bedding, and blackout curtains.

Entertainment Options: Provide a variety of entertainment options such as board games, streaming services, and books.

3. Create a Theme for Your Unit

A themed unit can make your Airbnb memorable and unique:

Consistency: Choose a theme that is consistent throughout the property, whether it's coastal, rustic, or modern.

Personal Touch: Incorporate personal touches and unique décor items that reflect the theme.

Appeal: A well-executed theme can attract guests looking for a unique experience.

4. Pick Fun Colors

Color can greatly impact the mood and appeal of your space:

Vibrant Accents: Use bold and fun colors for accent walls, furniture, and décor items to create a lively atmosphere.

Cohesive Palette: Ensure that the colors you choose complement each other and fit the overall theme of your property.

Inviting Spaces: Bright, cheerful colors can make spaces feel more welcoming and enjoyable.

5. Add Travel Size Amenities for Guests

Small details can make a big difference in guest satisfaction:

Convenience: Provide travel-size toiletries like shampoo, conditioner, body wash, and lotion.

Thoughtfulness: Guests appreciate thoughtful touches such as makeup remover wipes, dental kits, and sewing kits.

First Impressions: These amenities create a positive first impression and demonstrate your attention to detail.

6. Have a Game Room Section

A dedicated game room can be a major draw for guests:

Variety: Include a variety of games such as a pool table, foosball, board games, and video game consoles.

Entertainment: A game room provides additional entertainment options, especially for families and groups.

Unique Selling Point: This feature can set your property apart from others in the area.

7. Have Coffee and Tea Available to Guests

Providing coffee and tea can enhance the guest experience:

Starter Packs: Offer a starter pack with a selection of coffee and tea, sugar, creamer, and even some snacks.

Equipment: Ensure there is a coffee maker, kettle, and appropriate cups and mugs.

Comfort: These small comforts can make guests feel more at home and appreciated.

8. List Your Number for 24/7 Contact

Being available to your guests can significantly improve their stay:

Accessibility: Provide your contact number and assure guests they can reach you anytime for assistance.

Responsiveness: Quick responses to inquiries or issues can lead to better reviews and repeat bookings.

Trust: Guests feel more secure knowing they can contact the host at any time.

9. Create a Map of Things in the Area

Help your guests explore the local area with ease:

Local Attractions: Highlight nearby attractions, restaurants, parks, and other points of interest.

Insider Tips: Include recommendations for lesser-known spots and local favorites.

Ease of Use: Provide a physical map and a digital version accessible via a QR code.

10. Brand, Brand, Brand

Branding your Airbnb can create a memorable experience and encourage repeat visits:

Consistent Theme: Develop a consistent theme that reflects your brand, from décor to amenities.

Personal Touch: Consider adding branded items like welcome notes, keychains, and custom toiletries.

Social Media: Create a social media presence for your Airbnb, encouraging guests to share their experiences and tag your property.

By implementing these strategies, you can create an Airbnb that stands out from the competition and provides an exceptional experience for your guests. A well-furnished, thoughtfully designed, and guest-focused property will not only attract more bookings but also encourage positive reviews and repeat visit.

11

THE END/YOUR NEW BEGINNING

Now that we have come to the end of this book, it is really the beginning for you. It is my sincere desire that you will use the information that I have given you in this book. Please use it to build your business credit, and, more importantly, to create your own lifestyle!

Before we wrap up, I want to leave you with one last secret, as well as share with you how you can manufacture spending.

One of the best and easiest ways to do this is through Stripe. To execute this, all you need to do is:

- Set up an account
- Invoice yourself
- Swipe your business credit card
- Use the funds to pay off any of your other cards
- And repeat!

This can also be done via PayPal or any merchant account. This process is also known, behind the scenes in the business world, as liquidating your credit card. The benefit of this process is that you can keep your rewards and utilize your business credit cards to help you build business credit.

Be sure to join Bosses Build Business Credit Group on Facebook if you're confused about anything laid out in this book. And always remember...

BOSSES BUILD BUSINESS CREDIT!
BONUS
Fifteen Verified Easy Approval
Net-30 Accounts and Vendors

1. The CEO Creative

The CEO Creative specializes in custom design and branding services but also carries products like electronics, office supplies, and apparel.

This makes their net-30 program a practical choice for many small business owners who are looking for affordable branding while simultaneously building business credit and boosting cash flow.

To qualify, you need to be a US-based business, have existed for at least 30 days, have a clean business credit history, and not have any late payment history.

Minimum orders needed to report to the credit bureau: $0

Membership fee per year: $49 to maintain net-30 account credit terms. Like most net-30 accounts, there are no interest rate charges.

Credit bureaus where transactions are reported:

- Dun & Bradstreet
- Equifax Business
- Creditsafe

Beneficial for businesses in these industries:

- B2B
- Medical
- Construction
- Manufacturing
- Restaurant supplies

2. JJ Gold International

Though JJGold International's product line of gift sets, decor products, jewelry, men's products, and eyewear won't apply to all businesses, their net-30 account bears mentioning.

They offer over 1,000 products and report to D&B and Experian Business, which can be instrumental in improving your business credit score while boosting cash flow.

To qualify for 30-day payment terms, you just need to be a US-based business, have operated for at least 30 days, and have a clean payment history with no late payments. Just note that JJ Gold International only offers net-30 terms on 50% of orders, and the other 50% must be paid upfront.

Minimum orders needed to report to the credit bureau: $100

Membership fee per year: $99 to maintain net-30 account payment terms

Credit bureaus where transactions are reported:

- Dun & Bradstreet
- Experian Business

Beneficial for businesses in these industries:

- Startups
- E-commerce businesses

3. Shogun Roasting

The new "no fee" net-30 account. Shogun Roasting is an exceptional coffee roasting company that has captured the hearts and palates of coffee enthusiasts around the globe. With a relentless dedication to quality and a deep respect for the art of roasting, Shogun Roasting has become synonymous with excellence in the coffee industry.

Minimum orders needed to report to the credit bureau:
After one prepaid order you can apply for a business account

- For transactions to be reported, your account must contain a balance at the end of the month. Note that credit card purchases and same-month payments are not reported.

Membership fee per year: $0 to maintain net-30 account credit terms

Credit bureaus where transactions are reported:

- Experian
- Dun & Bradstreet
- Equifax
- Credit Safe

Beneficial for businesses in these industries:

- Home office
- Hospitality
- Healthcare
- Under ten employees

4. Wise Business Plans

Wise Business Plans provides various services relating to business plans and formations, business website design, business license searches, branding, digital marketing, business compliance, and others.

Businesses that want to apply for a net-30 credit line with Wise Business Plans must have a valid tax ID number or Employer Identification Number, be filed with the Secretary of State, and have no major business delinquencies. Applications are reviewed within 24 business hours, at which point the account will receive an initial credit limit.

Businesses that have qualified for a net-30 account will receive an approval email. The starter credit limit can grow over time if you have regular transactions with Wise Business Plans and make on-time payments. Additionally, net-30 accounts are reported monthly to credit bureaus. (See our Wise Business Plans Net-30 Review article for more details.)

Minimum orders needed to report to the credit bureau: $97

Membership fee per year: $99 to maintain net-30 account credit terms

Credit bureaus where transactions are reported:

- Experian
- Equifax
- Dun & Bradstreet
- Creditsafe

2

Beneficial for businesses in these industries:

- Local businesses
- Startups
- Franchises
- E-commerce businesses

5. NAMYNOT

As a digital marketing services firm, NAMYNOT offers a variety of online business marketing solutions such as SEO, social media marketing, content marketing, inbound lead generation, video production, and more.

Aside from having an Employer Identification Number, businesses that want to apply for a net-30 account with NAMYNOT must be established for at least 90 days, have a clean credit history, be registered in their respective states with good standing, and have a professional website, not a "Coming Soon" one.

NAMYNOT also offers credit lines that can go up to $10,000, and the approval process can take five to ten business days.

Minimum orders needed to report to the credit bureau: $0

Membership fee per year: $0 to maintain net-30 account credit terms

Credit bureau where transactions are reported:

- Dun & Bradstreet

Beneficial for businesses in these industries:

- Telcos
- Online businesses or e-commerce shops
- Boutiques
- Tech companies or startups

6. Business T-Shirt Club

Unlike other companies selling apparel, the Business T-Shirt Club is exclusively for business owners and entrepreneurs. The company is membership-based wherein members can have access to high-quality apparel brands at wholesale rates. You will only be charged for custom print design and services.

Accounts that are approved for a net-30 billing will have their activities with Business T-Shirt Club reported every month.

Minimum orders needed to report to the credit bureau: 50% deposit on all orders for new members, which will be lifted after a minimum of five orders with no late or outstanding balances

Membership fee per year: $89.99 to maintain net-30 account credit terms

Credit bureaus where transactions are reported:

- Cortera
- Ansonia
- Equifax
- Experian
- Dun & Bradstreet
- Creditsafe

Beneficial for businesses in these industries:

- Retail businesses
- Hospitality
- Companies with field representatives

7. Creative Analytics

Focusing on growth marketing, web design, branding, and automation, Creative Analytics has a lot to offer B2B companies.

With nearly 20 years of experience and after serving over 22,000 clients, this net-30 vendor has a proven track record and strives to "captivate, convince, and convert audiences."

Note that this vendor has two net-30 account options for building business credit. You can pay $79 annually for an initial credit limit of $1,000. Or you can pay $49–$149 per month for an initial credit limit of $12,000.

To qualify for net-30 payment terms, you must be US-based, have been in business for at least 30 days, and not have any derogatory payment remarks.

Minimum orders needed to report to the credit bureaus: $100

Membership fee per year: $79 to maintain net-30 account credit terms, with an initial credit limit of $1,000 (there's also an option to pay $49 - $149 per month and get an initial credit limit of up to $12,000)

Credit bureaus where transactions are reported:

- Equifax Business
- Creditsafe

Beneficial for businesses in these industries:

- B2B companies
- Nonprofits

8. Office Garner

From office supplies and electronics to apparel and branded business cards and websites, Office Garner has everything small business owners need to get off the ground.

They have a simple one-time $69 fee to participate in their net-30 program (rather than a recurring annual fee).

And with reasonable eligibility requirements of operating in the US, being in business for just 30 days, and having a clean business history, Office Garner is a net-30 vendor many companies will be interested in.

Minimum orders needed to report to the credit bureau: $45

Membership fee per year: A one-time fee of $69 to maintain 30-day net terms

Credit bureaus where transactions are reported:

- Equifax Business
- Creditsafe

Beneficial for businesses in these industries:

- B2B
- Startups
- E-commerce businesses

9. Newegg Business

Some of Newegg Business's product categories include: computers, electronics, office supplies, networking solutions, and digital signage.

Therefore, there are several products you can conveniently purchase from Newegg Business to run your company while also building business credit and raising your credit score.

Applying for a net-30 account is straightforward. You simply need to have a registered business name and address, federal tax ID, DUNS number, and a Newegg Business account.

Minimum orders needed to report to the credit bureau: $0

Membership fee per year: $0 to maintain net-30 account credit terms

Credit bureaus where transactions are reported:

- Dun & Bradstreet
- Equifax Business

Beneficial for businesses in these industries:

- Startups
- Education
- Healthcare

10. Wayfair

With a staggering 40 million-plus products, including furniture, appliances, decor, lighting, and much more, Wayfair carries a massive catalog for businesses.

An added plus is that they offer frequent sales and discounts as well as fast and free shipping on orders over $35. They also have excellent customer service.

Note that, technically, Wayfair has a net 60 account, which gives you 60 days to pay an invoice. But it's included here because they offer at least 30-day payment terms.

Minimum orders needed to report to the credit bureau: $0

Membership fee per year: $0 to maintain net-30 account payment terms

Credit bureaus where transactions are reported:

- Dun & Bradstreet
- Experian Business

Beneficial for businesses in these industries:

- Startups
- B2B
- Anyone who needs office furniture or decor

11. HD Supply

If you're looking for a large variety of products, including office supplies, appliances, furniture, electronics, and more, you can have them all with HD Supply.

They have discounts on clearance items and discontinued items, as well as other promotions, which can be especially helpful for small businesses with tight budgets.

HD Supply has no membership fee or minimum order to be eligible for net-30 payment terms, making them stand out against many other vendors.

Minimum orders needed to report to the credit bureau: $0

Membership fee per year: $0 to maintain net-30 account payment terms

Credit bureau where transactions are reported:

- Dun & Bradstreet

Beneficial for businesses in these industries:

- Startups
- Hospitality
- Healthcare

12. Strategic Network Solutions

Strategic Network Solutions focuses on four main types of business services—business continuity, disaster recovery, endpoint security, and proactive support. Besides that, they carry computer accessories and office supplies, for well-rounded offerings.

To qualify, you must spend at least $90 on a downloadable product, and Strategic Network Solutions will give you a $2,000 credit limit on a net-30 account.

Minimum orders needed to report to the credit bureau: $90

Membership fee per year: $0 to maintain net-30 account payment terms

Credit bureaus where transactions are reported:

- Experian Business
- Creditsafe

Beneficial for businesses in these industries:

- E-commerce businesses
- B2B
- Startups

13. SupplyWorks

With SupplyWorks, you can find a nice selection of cleaning/janitorial, paper, HVAC, and lighting products while also increasing cash flow and raising your business credit score. Therefore, this vendor can be a good option when it comes to the nuts and bolts of running a brick-and-mortar.

The only downside is their $150 minimum order is higher than many other net-30 vendors, and they don't disclose which business credit bureaus they report to.

Minimum orders needed to report to the credit bureau: $150

Membership fee per year: $0 to maintain net-30 account credit terms

Credit bureau where transactions are reported is not disclosed.

Beneficial for businesses in these industries:

- Any brick-and-mortar business
- Hospitality
- Healthcare
- Education

14. Staples

As one of the world's leading suppliers of office products, Staples needs no introduction, and they're a consistent favorite among many business owners.

Besides office supplies, they also carry computers, electronics, printers, cleaning supplies, and more, making Staples a true one-stop shop. An added plus is that Staples gives you 5% back on purchases, and they have great customer service.

Minimum orders needed to report to the credit bureau: $0

Membership fee per year: $79–$299 per year, depending on the membership tier to maintain net-30 account credit terms

Business credit bureau reporting to:

- un & Bradstreet

Beneficial for businesses in these industries:

- Ten or more employees
- Any brick-and-mortar business
- Retail
- Education

15. Laughlin and Associates

Finally, Laughlin and Associates provide several business services, including accounting, taxes, compliance assistance, name changes, and trademark acquisition.

This makes this net-30 vendor ideal for startups that want to build credit while getting professional assistance during the initial business formation stages.

As long as you have a business bank account, a DUNS number, and are in good standing with the Secretary of State, you should be eligible for a net-30 account with Laughlin and Associates.

Minimum orders needed to report to the credit bureau: $0

Membership fee per year: $99 to maintain net-30 account payment terms

Credit bureaus where transactions are reported:

- Equifax Business
- Experian Business

Beneficial for businesses in these industries:

- Startups
- E-commerce businesses
- Most companies in the business formation stage

AIRBNB EIN ONLY

Business Development & No PG Business Credit
Patrice S. Jordan, No PG Business Credit Consultant
Address: 6543 S. Las Vegas Blvd., Las Vegas, NV 89119
Phone: 844-478-2858
www.bossesbuildbusinesscredit.com

To order additional copies of *Airbnb EIN Only*:
www.Patricebookoffer.com
Bulk orders are available!

Patrice is available for One-on-One Business Coaching and
Consultations as well as speaking engagements, seminars, and
workshops. **Book Patrice S. Jordan for a Speaking Event:**
Bookings@patricesjordan.com
www.patricesjordan.com

YOUTUBE   BOOKINGS

SCAN ME

www.ingramcontent.com/pod-product-compliance
Lightning Source LLC
Chambersburg PA
CBHW061042110426
42740CB00050B/2847